Giraffe

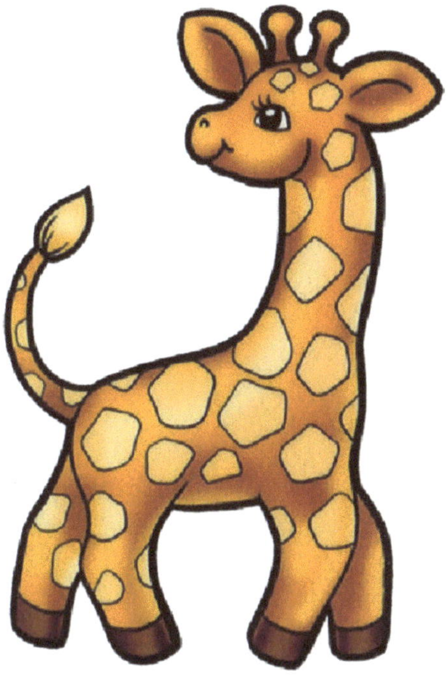

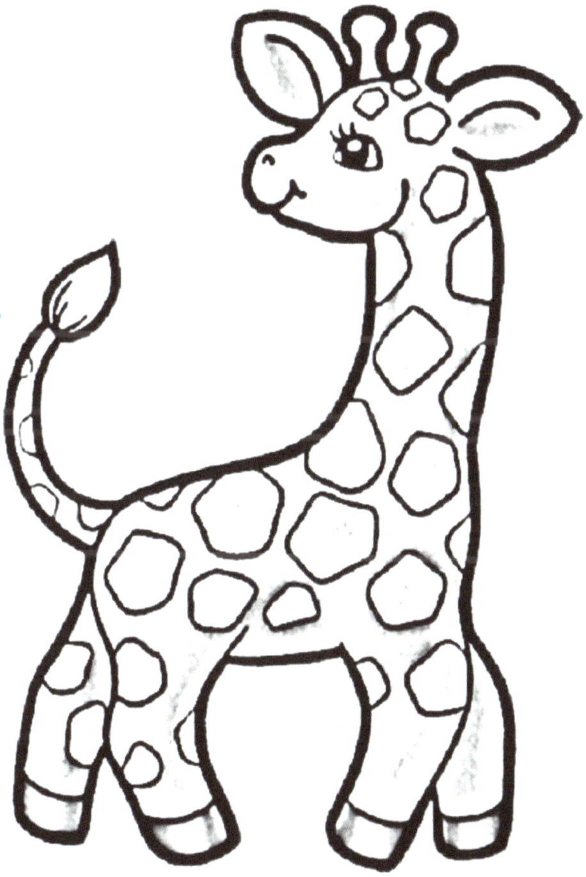

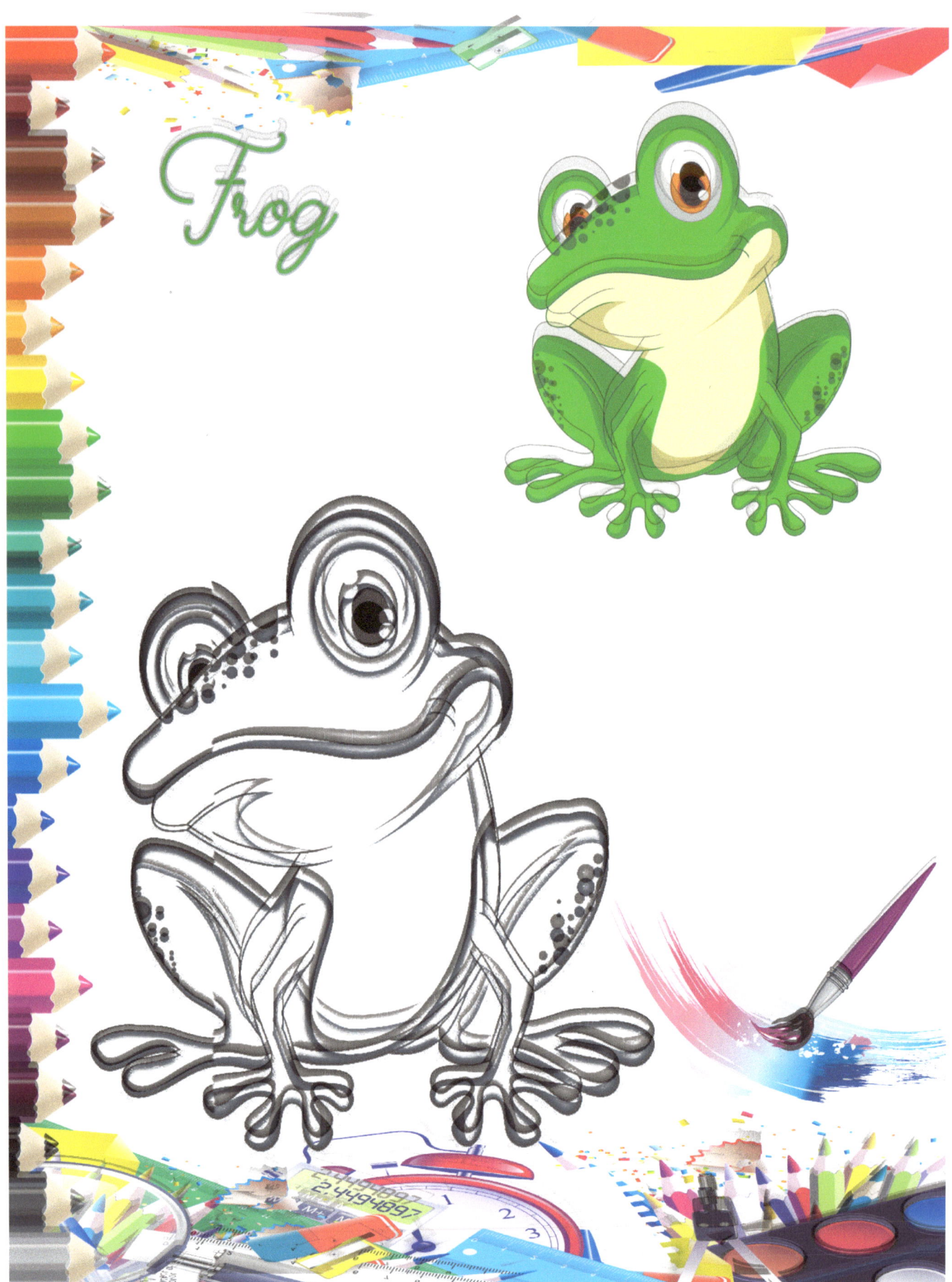

Frog

Kitten

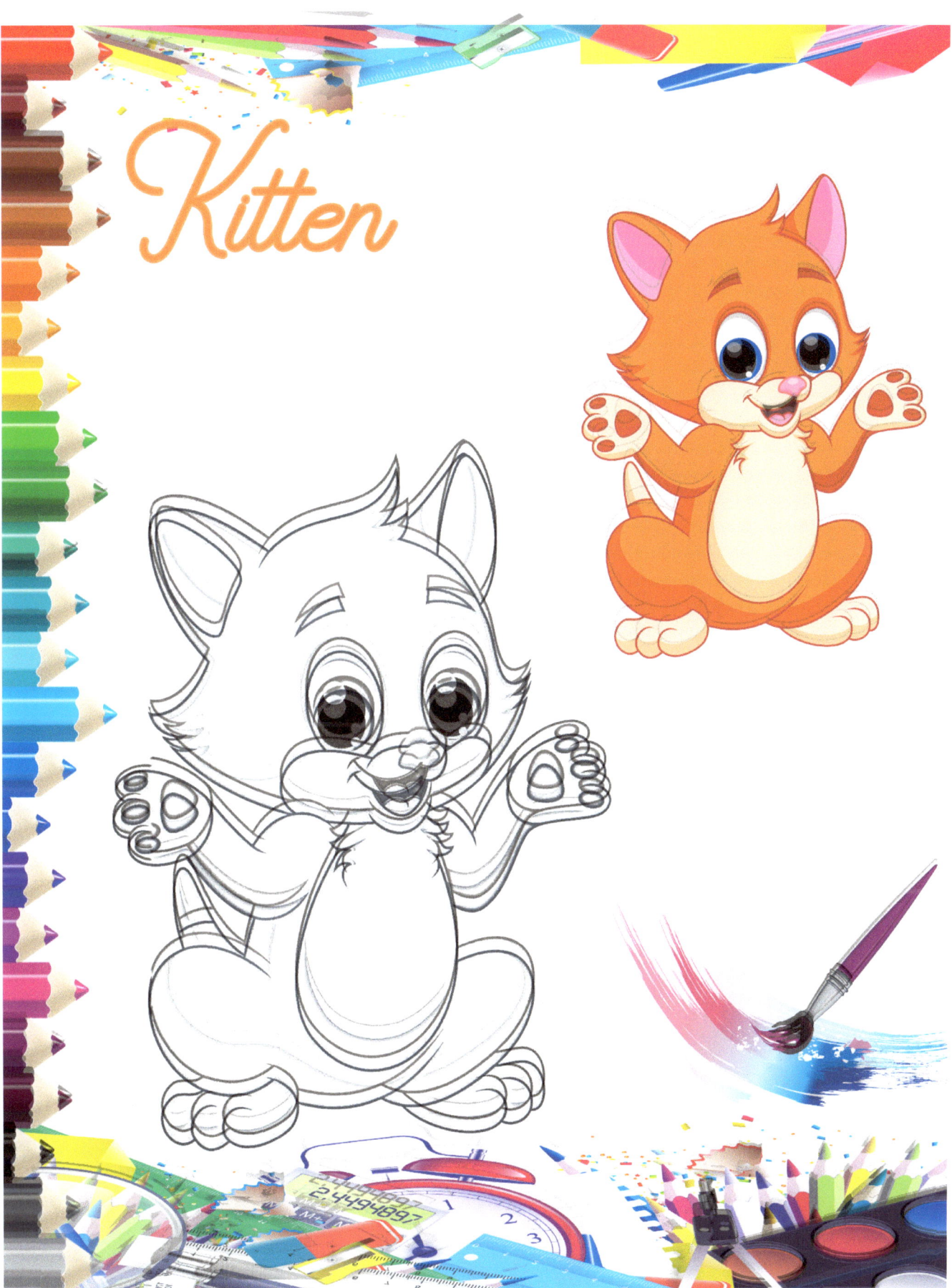

Elephant

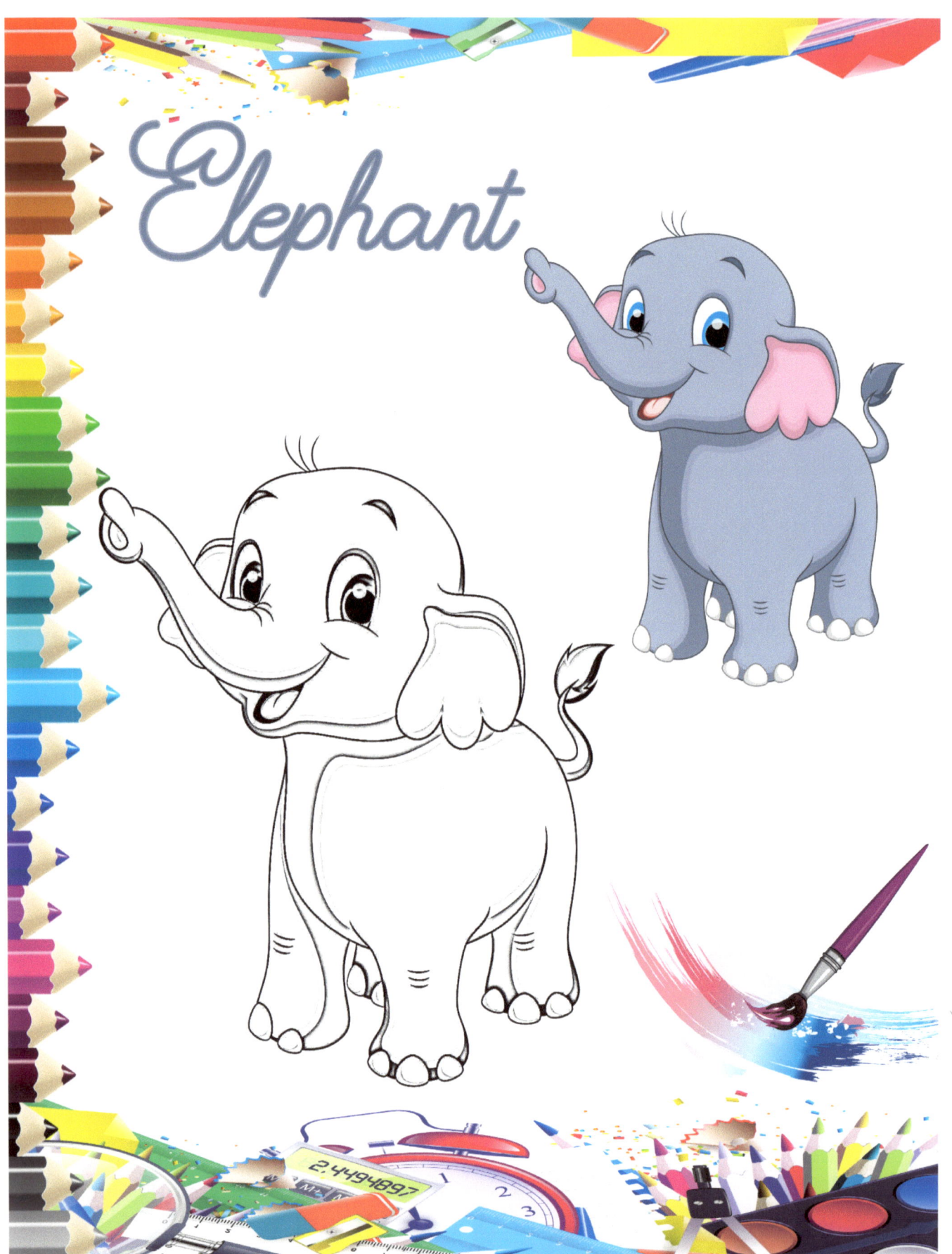

Dog

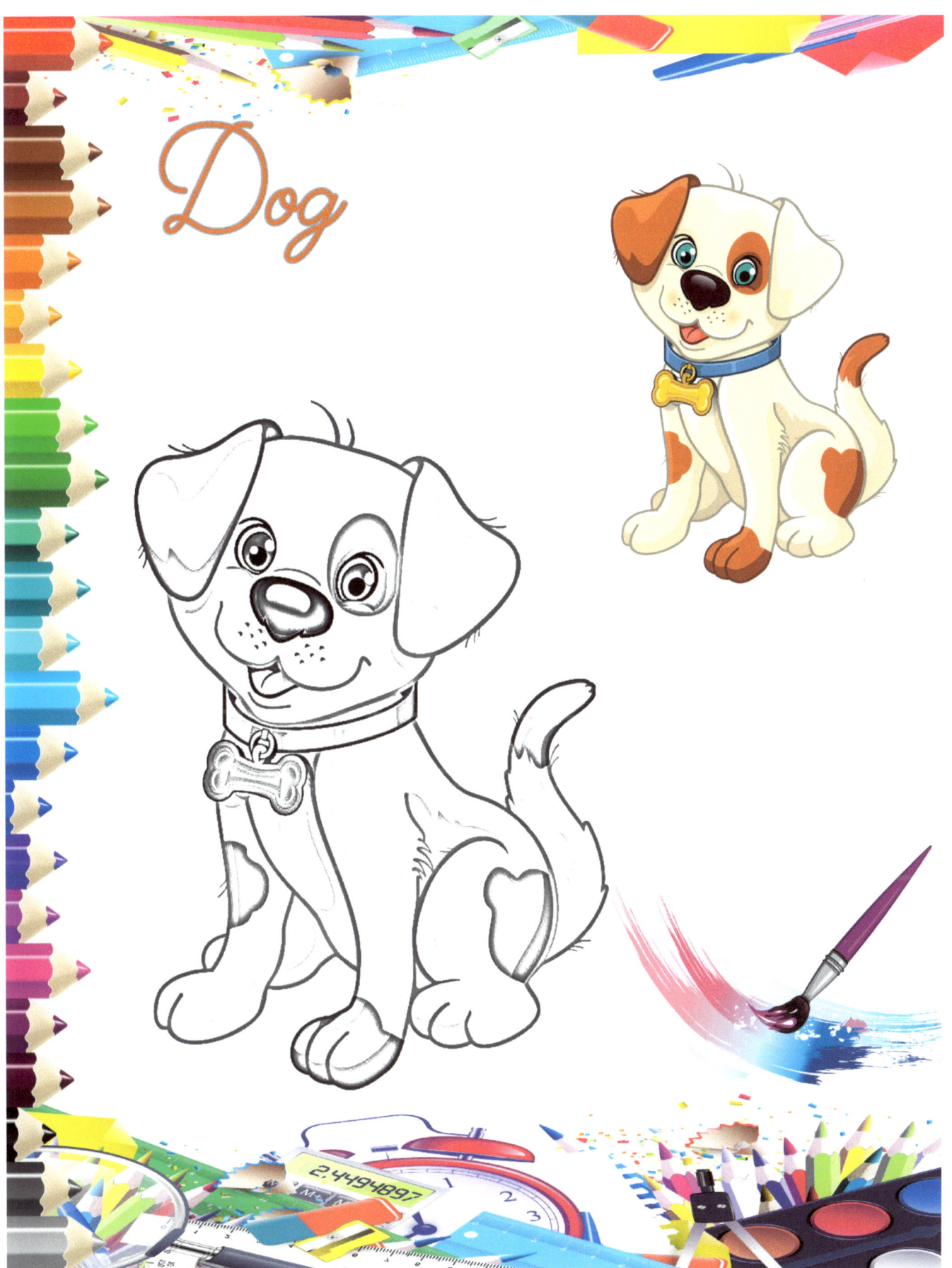

Butterfly

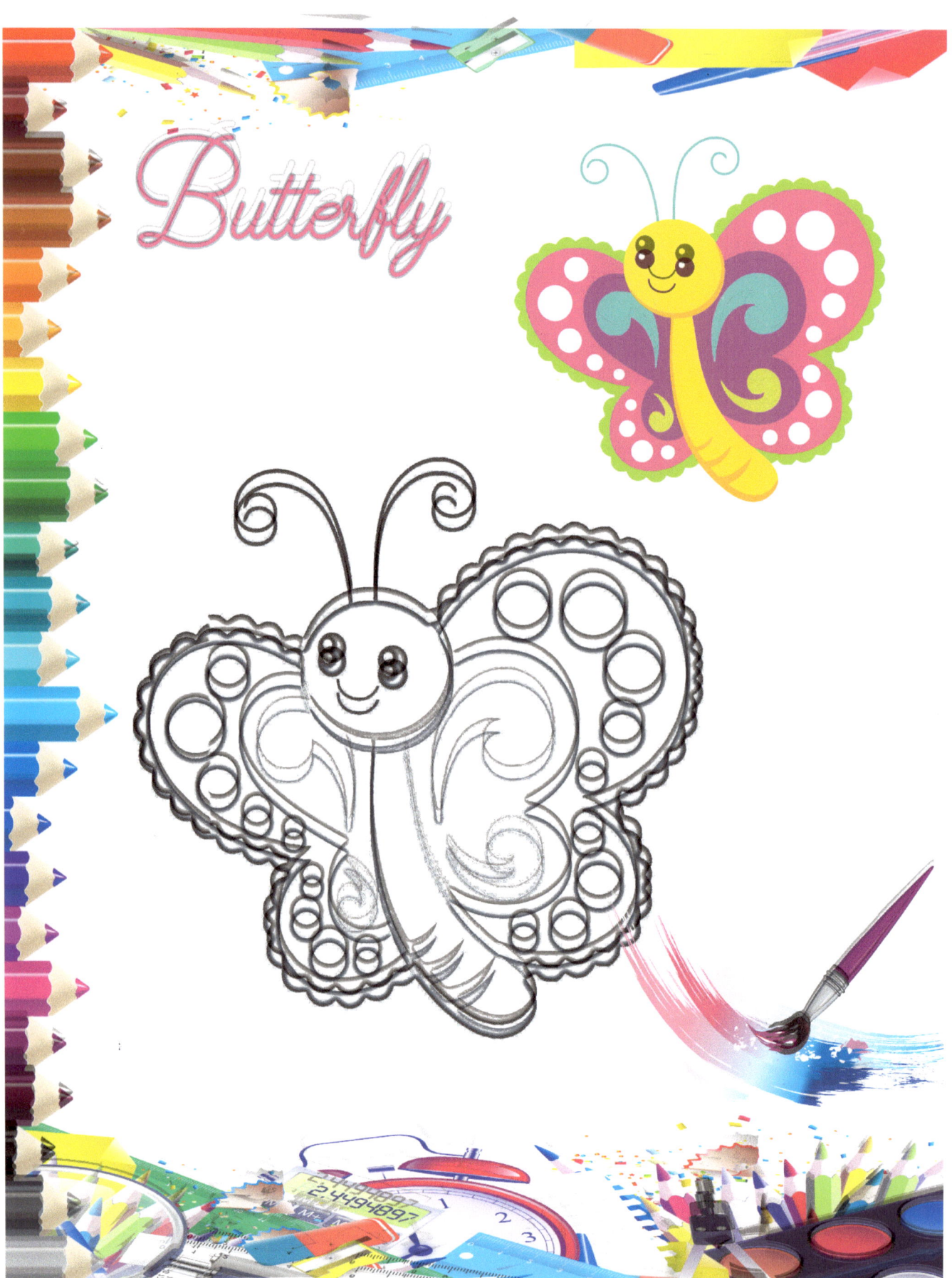

Ant

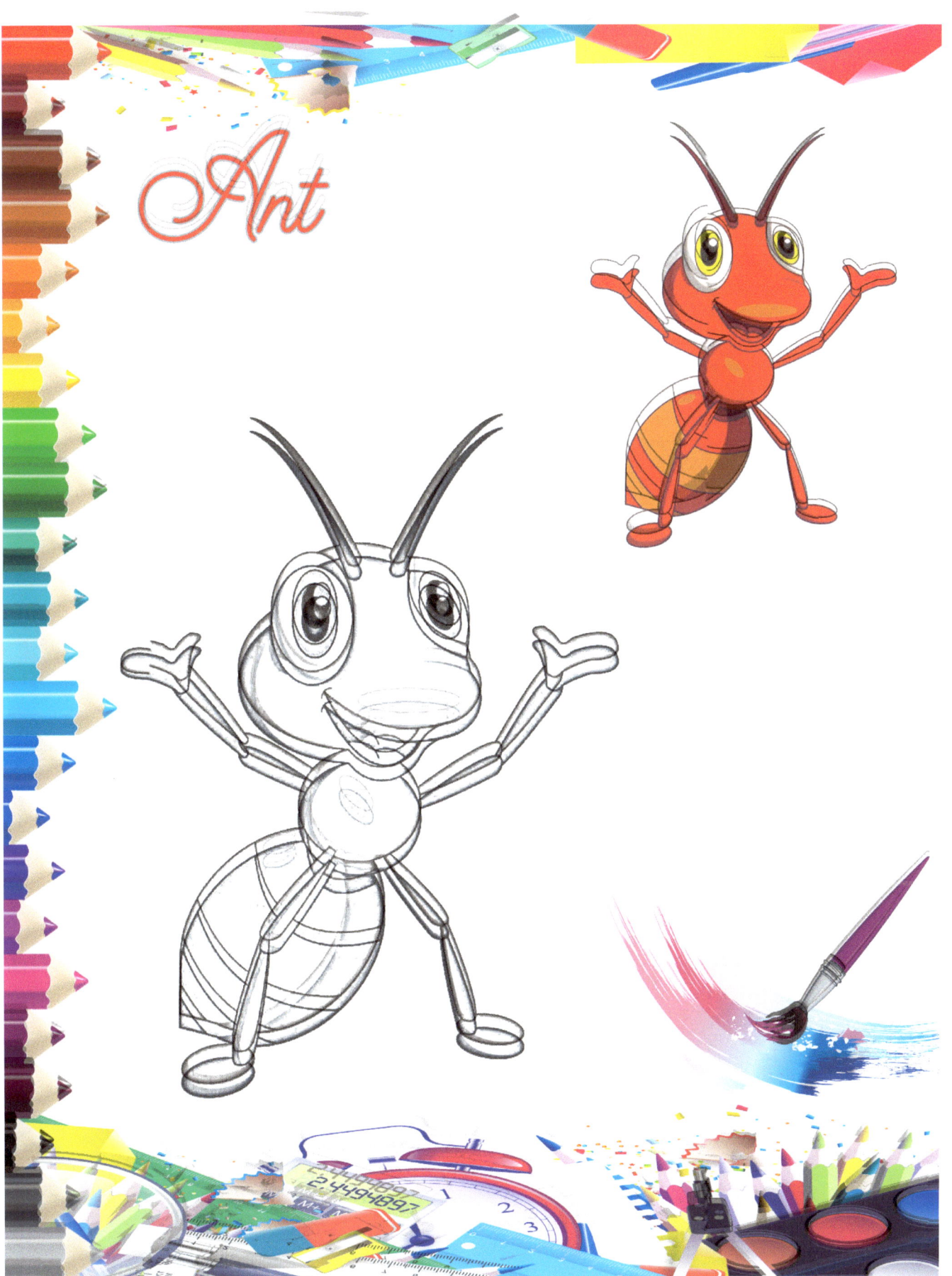

Deer

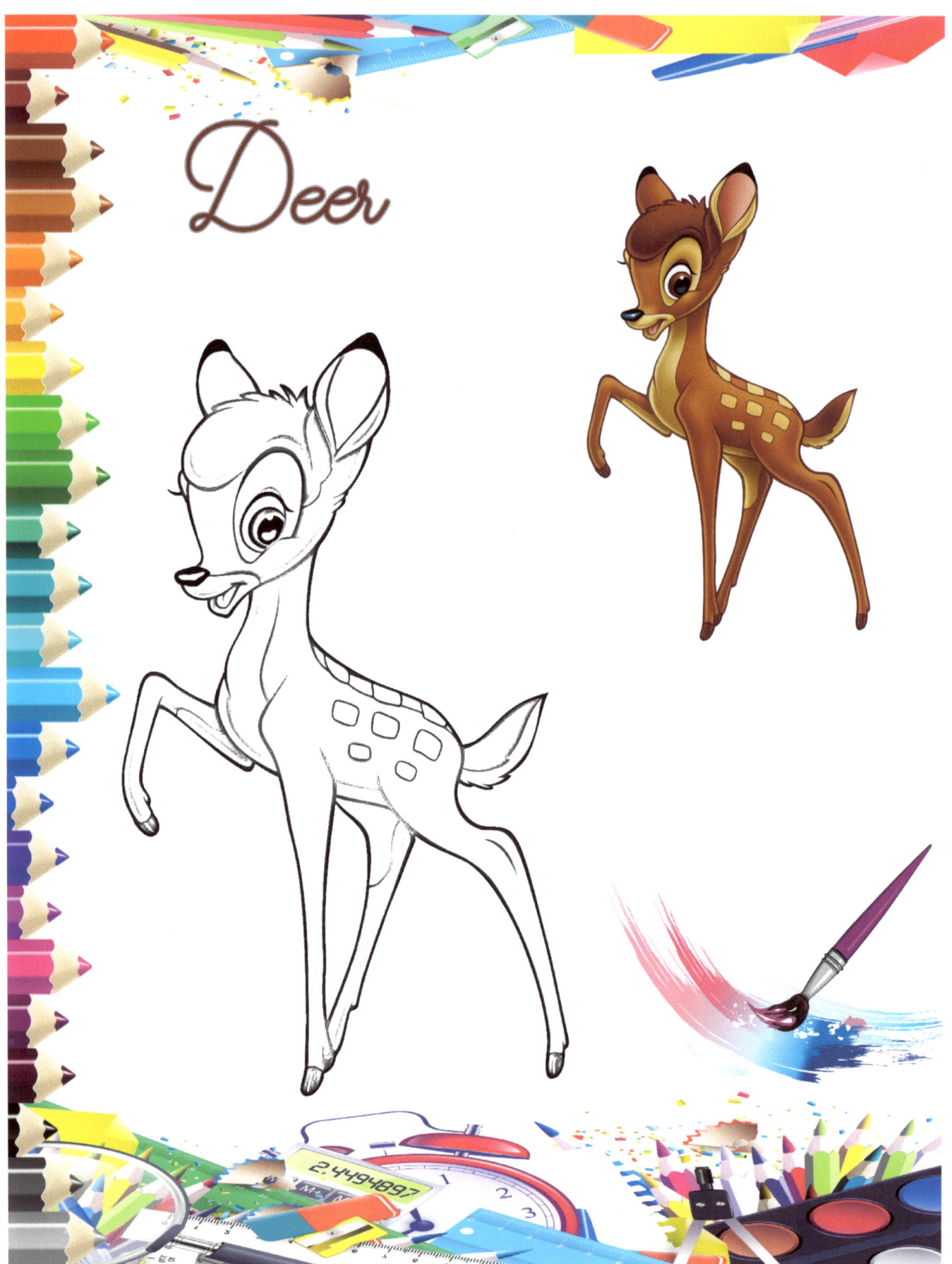

Cow

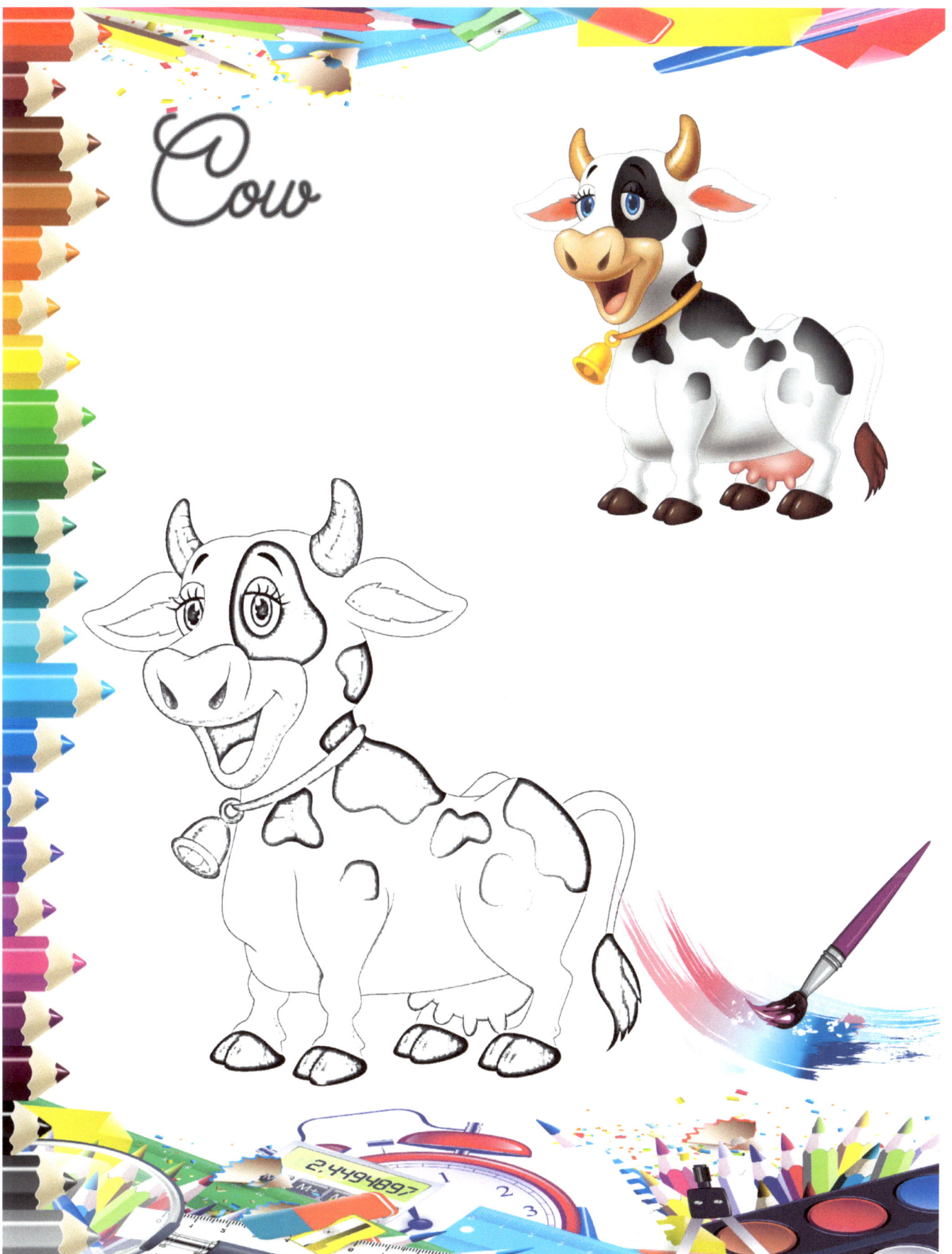

Snake

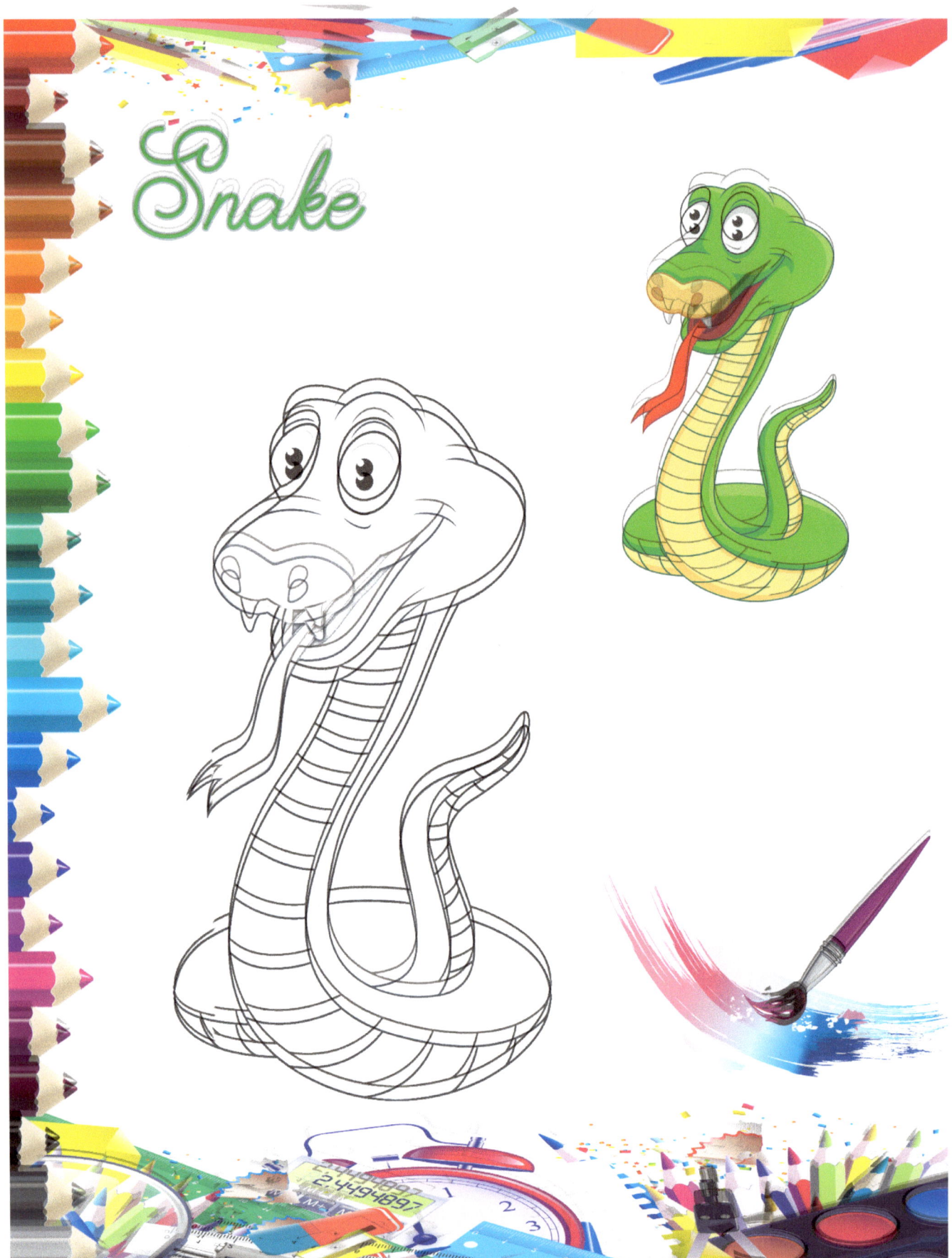

Dolphin

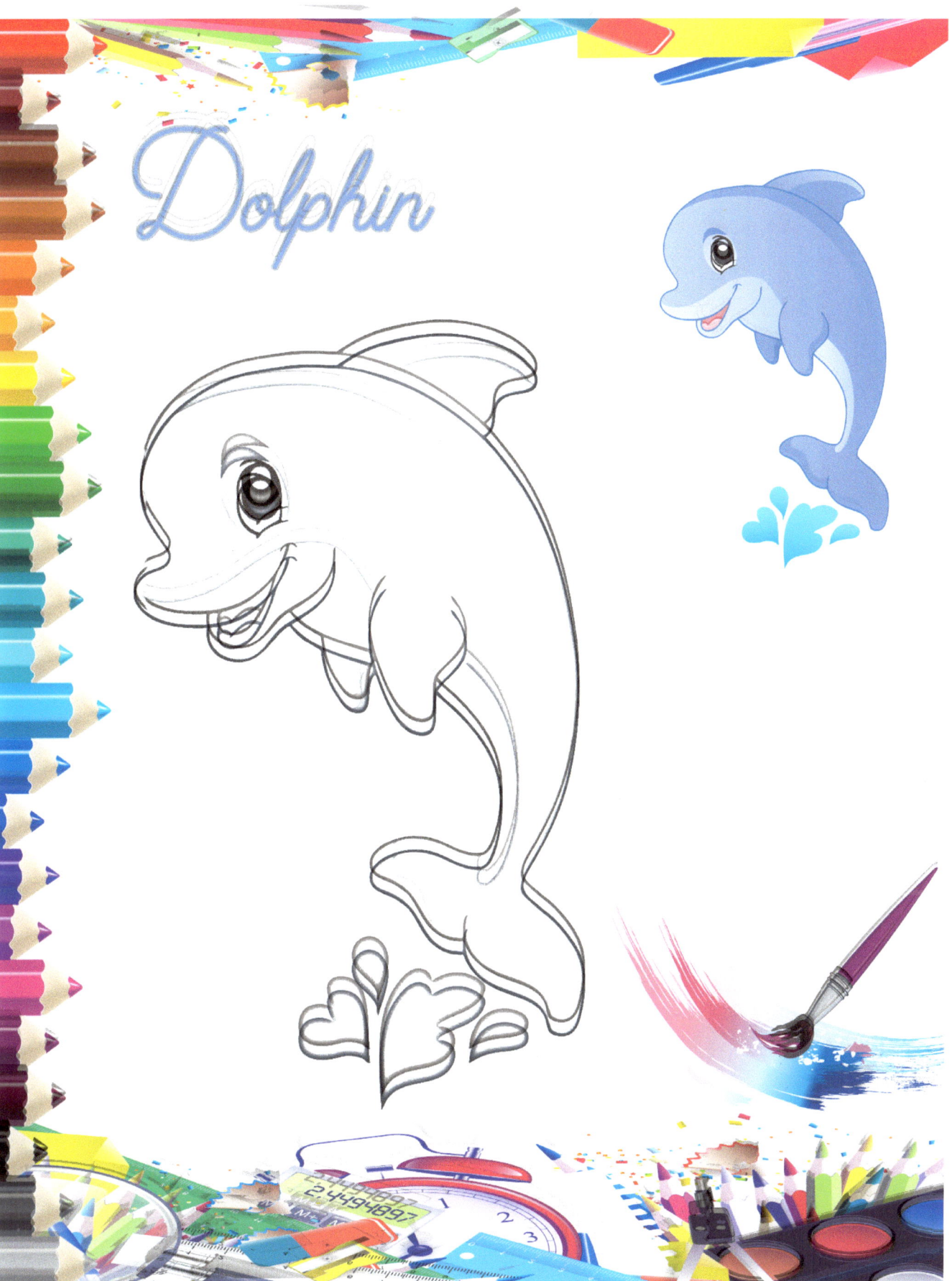

Monkey

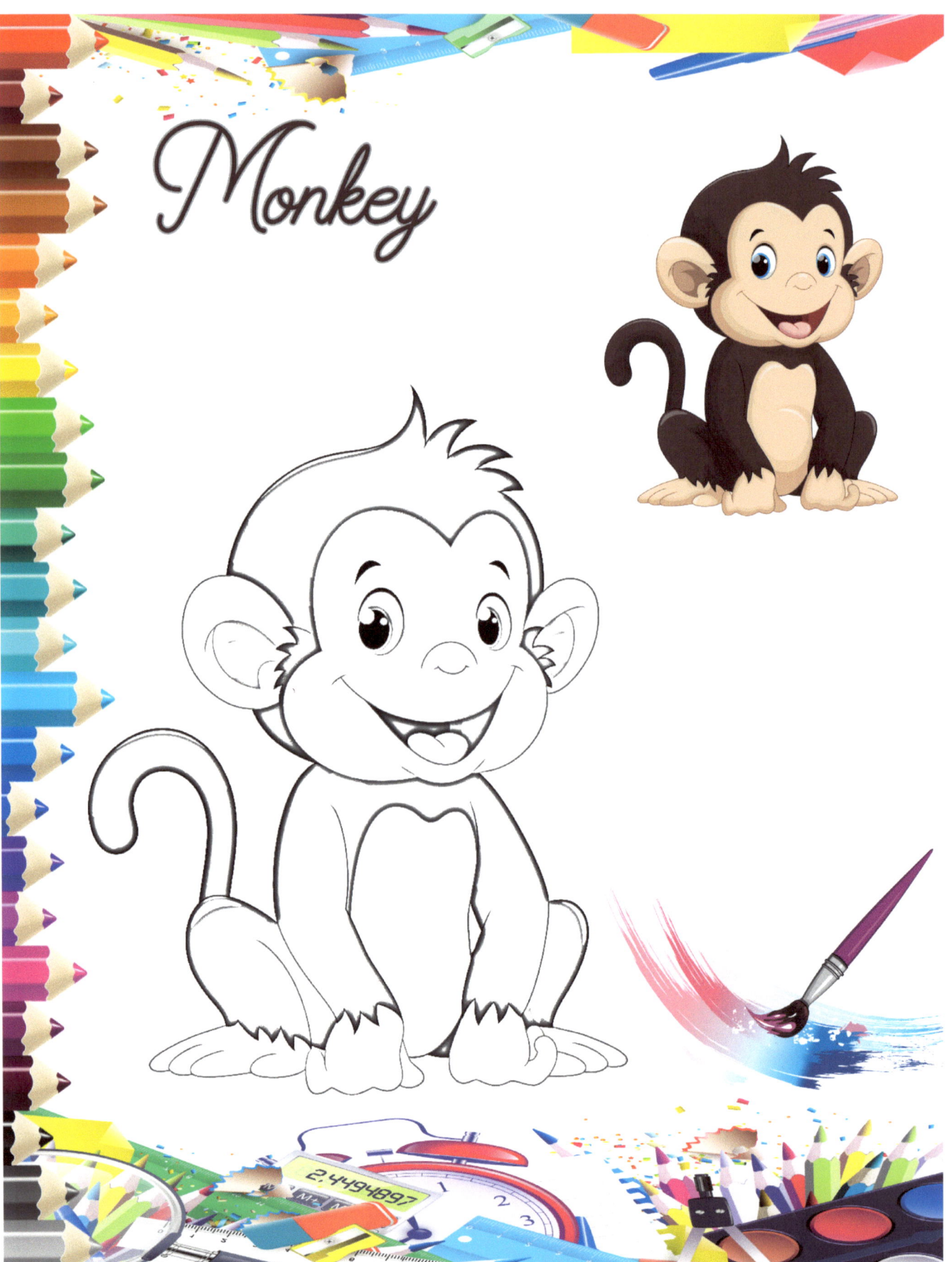

Fish

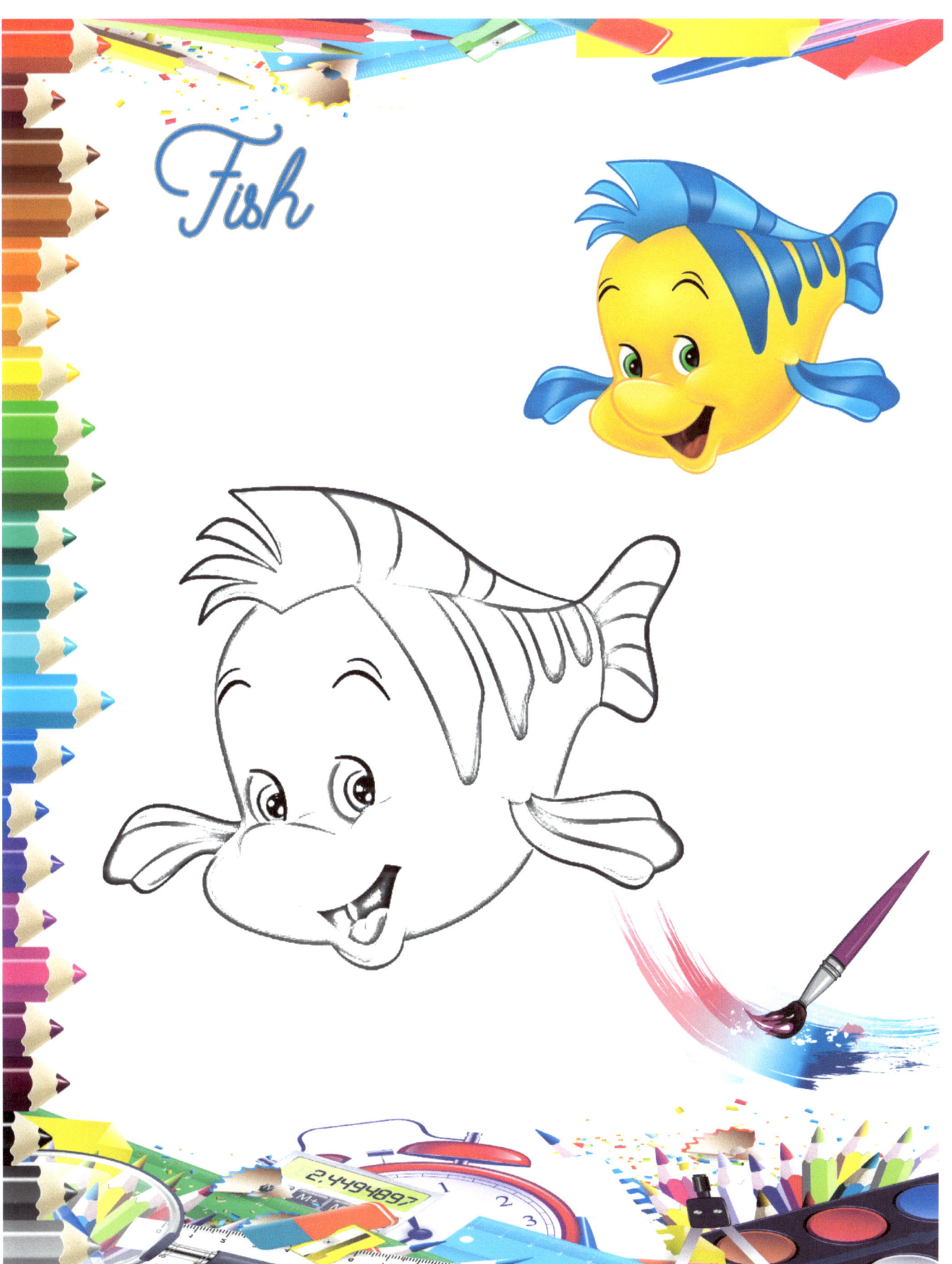

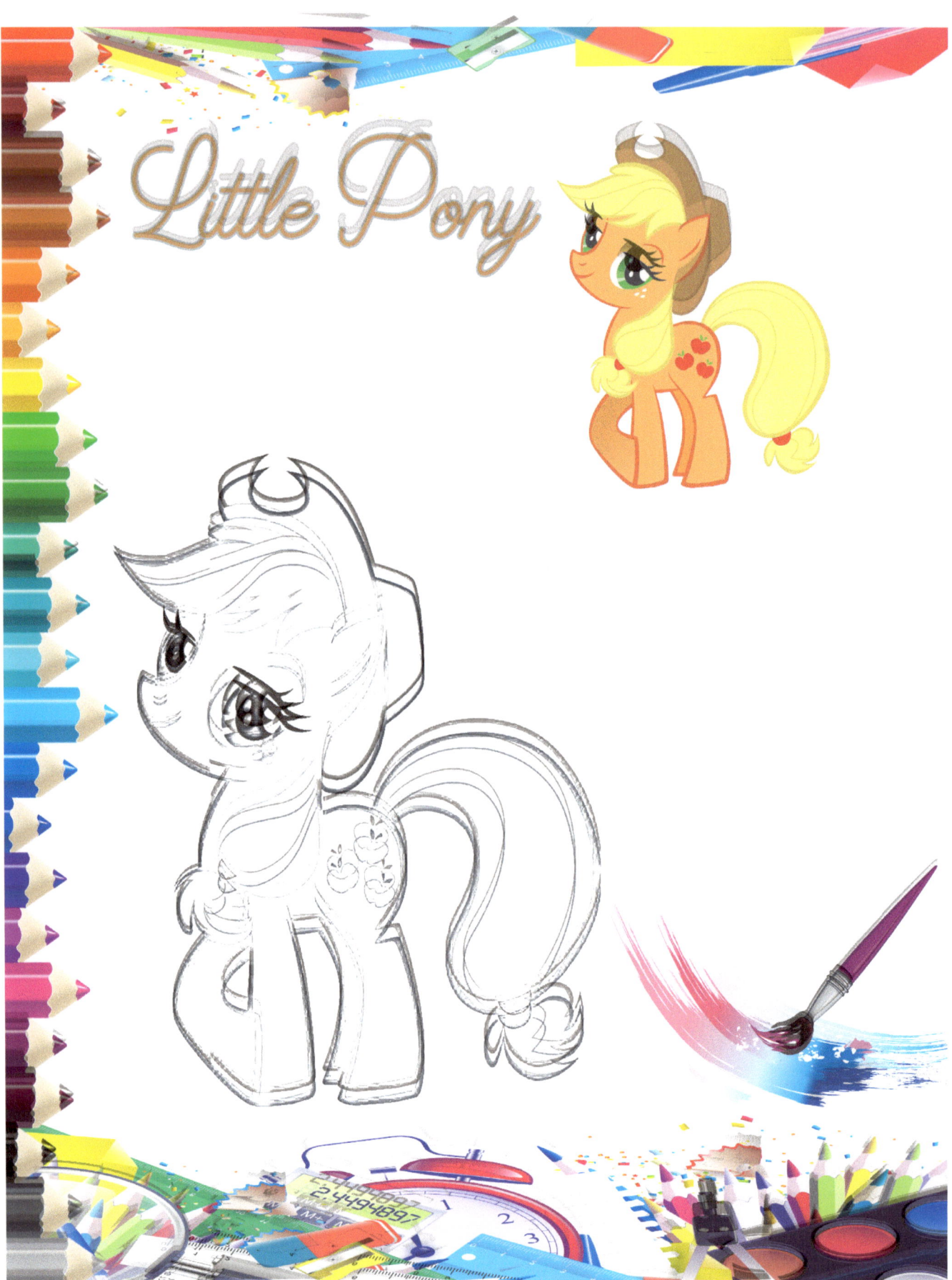

Parrot

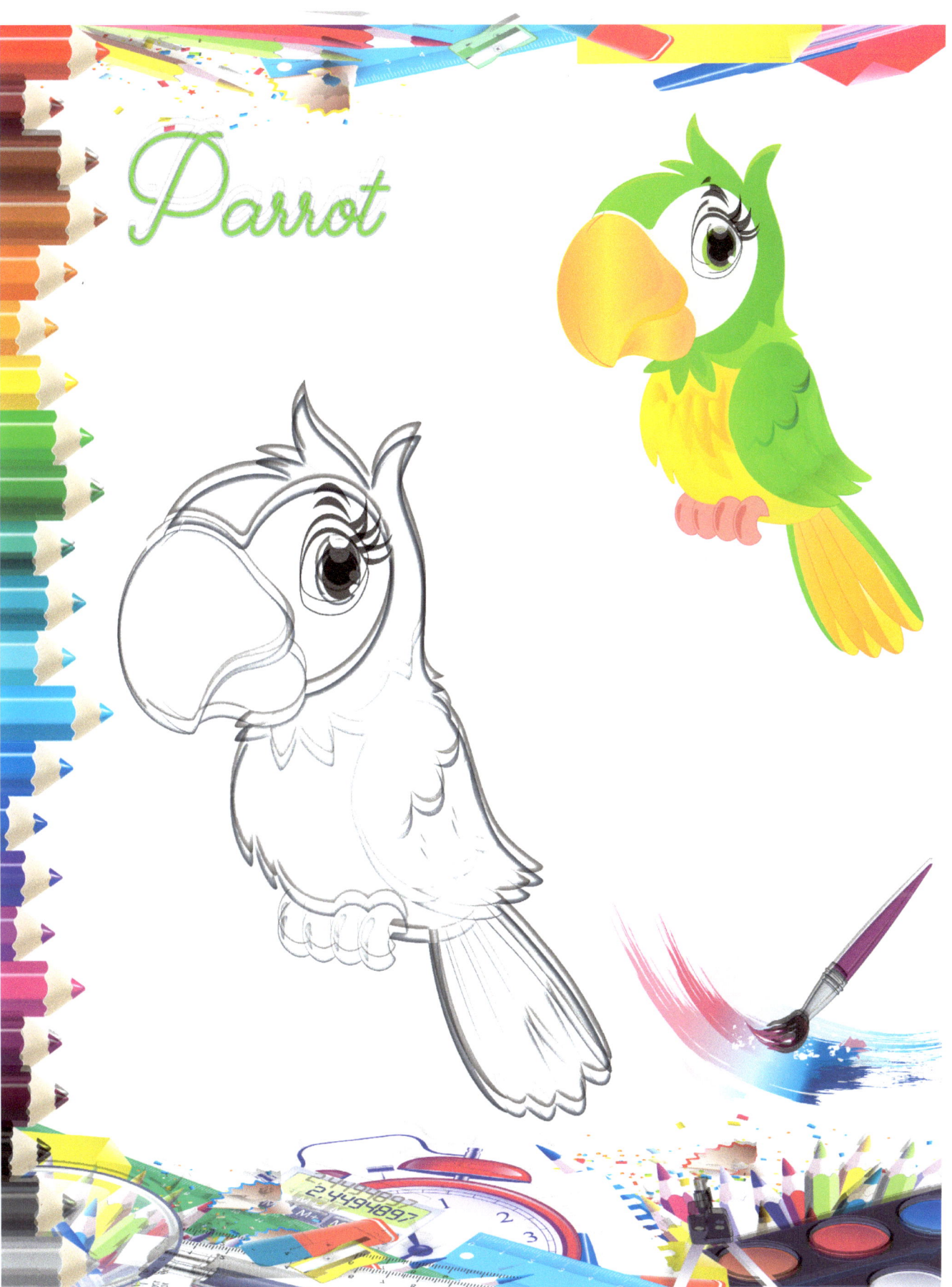

Owl

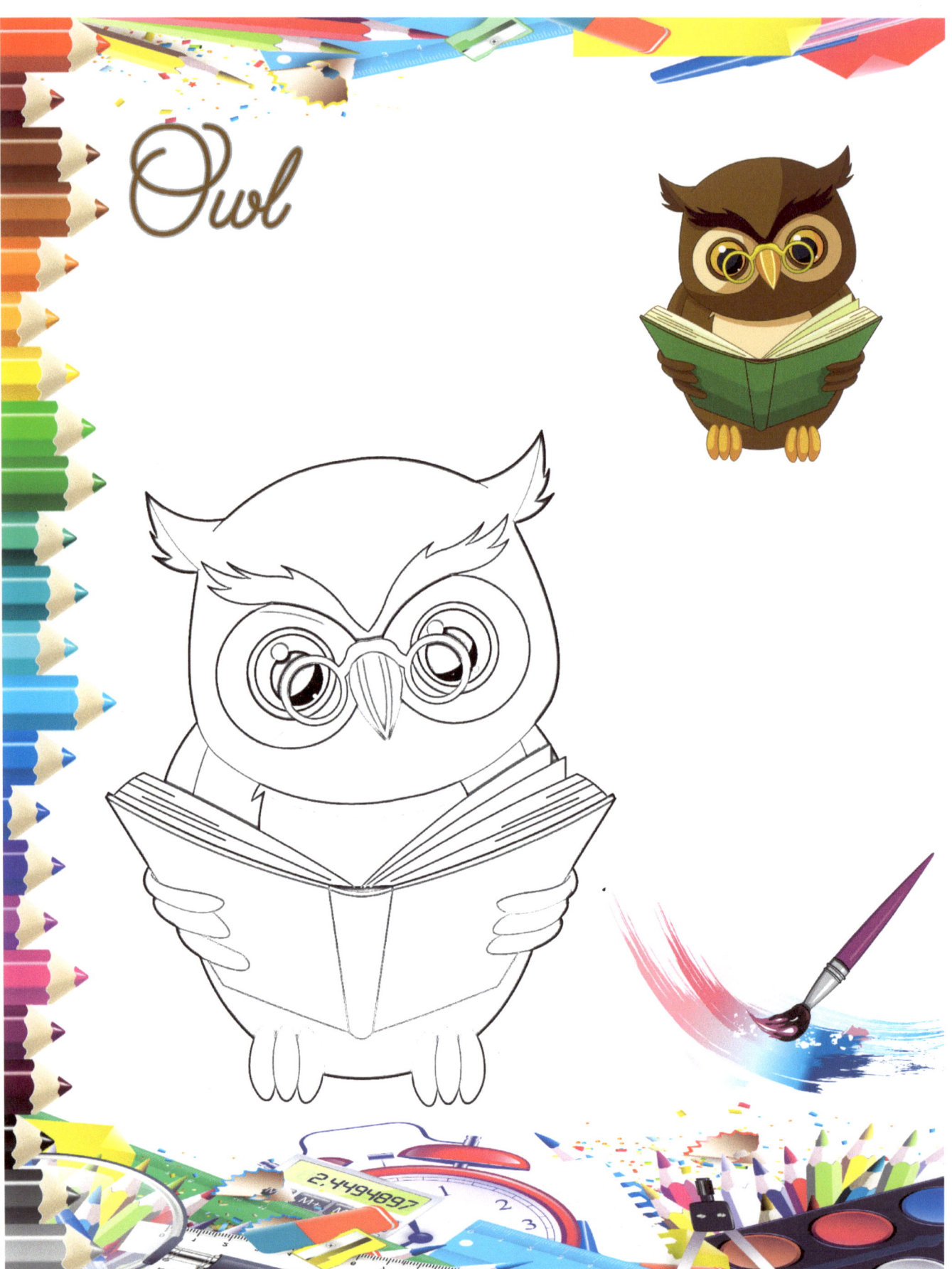

Cock

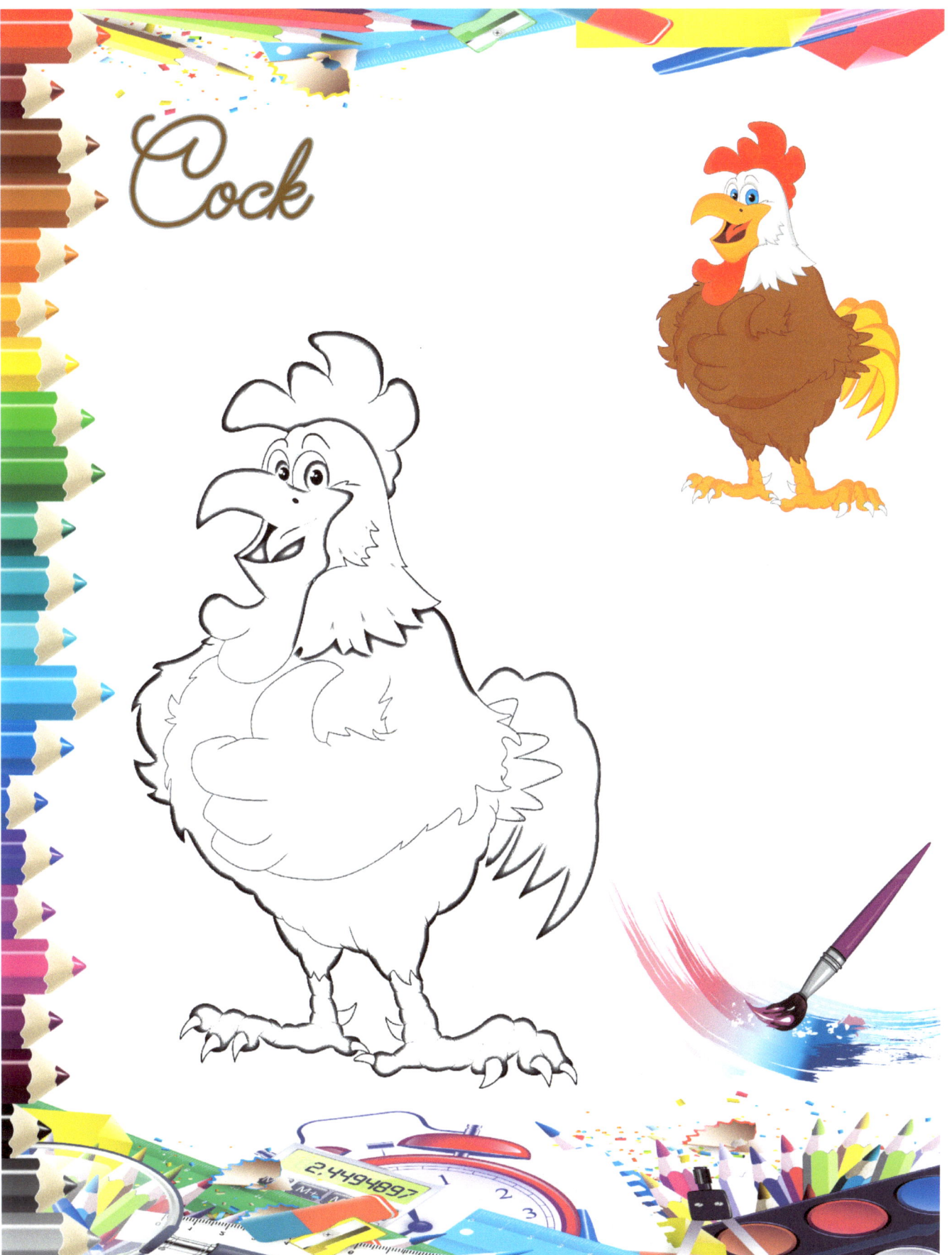

Kangaroo

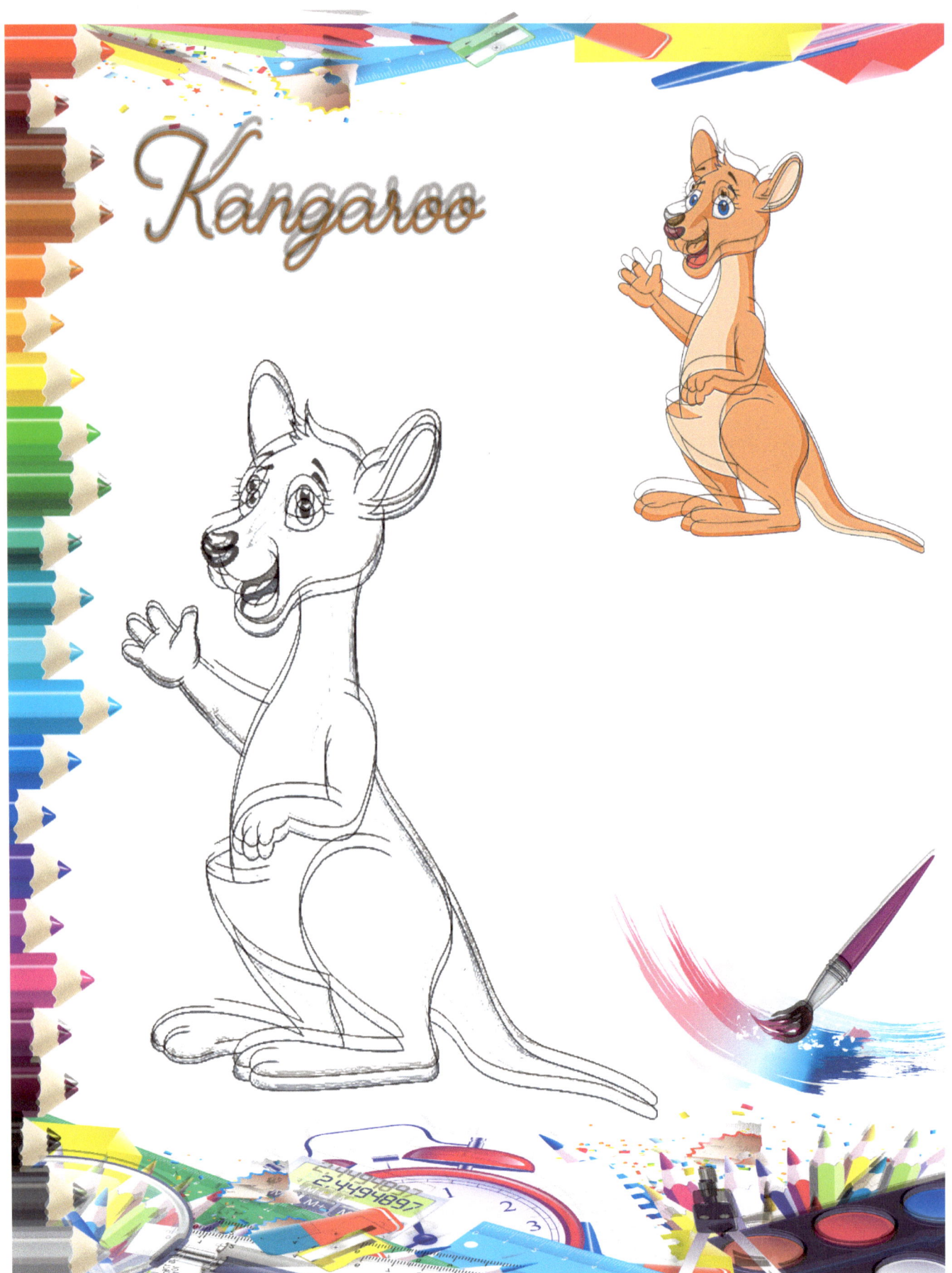

Lion

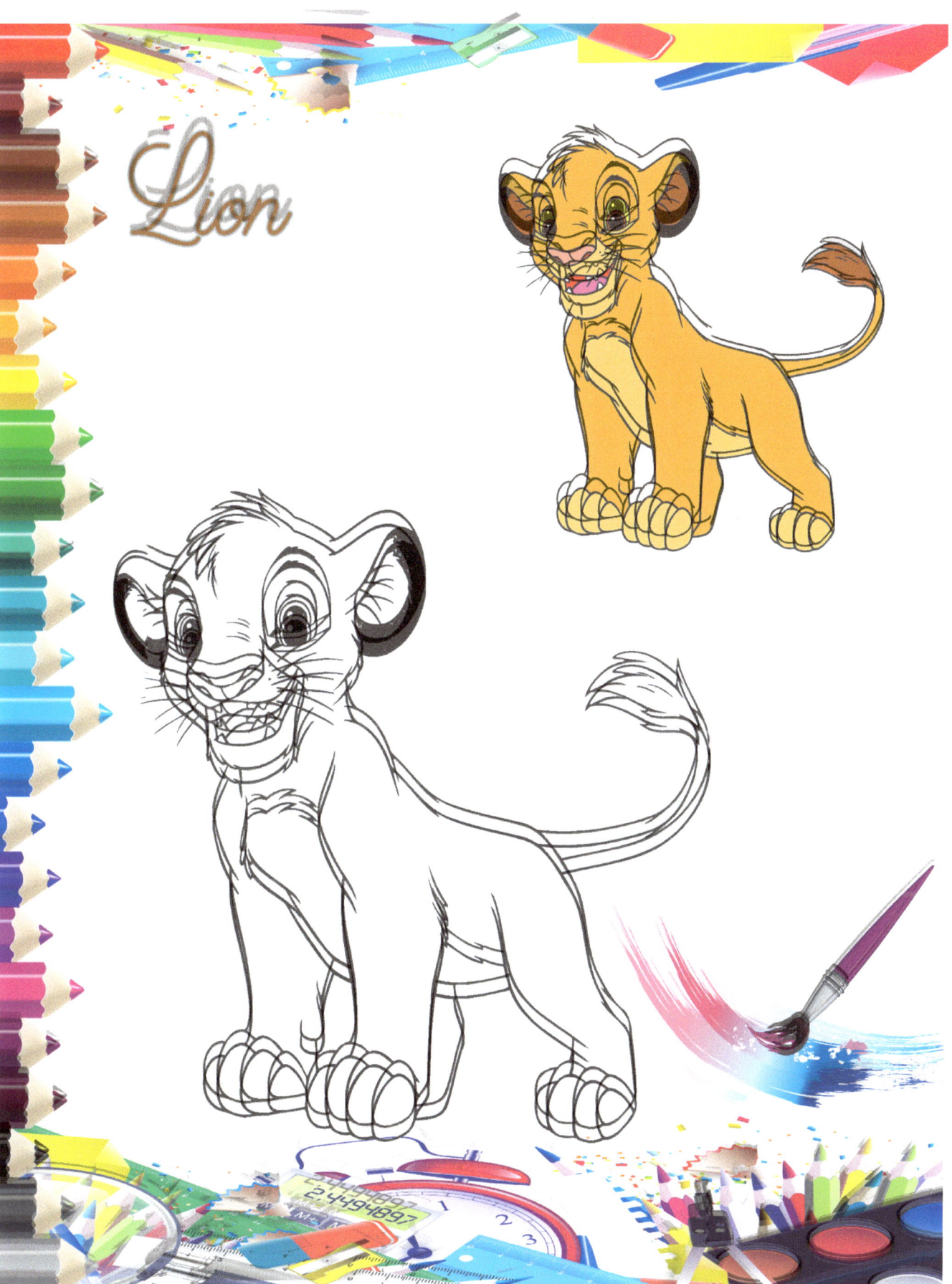

Goat

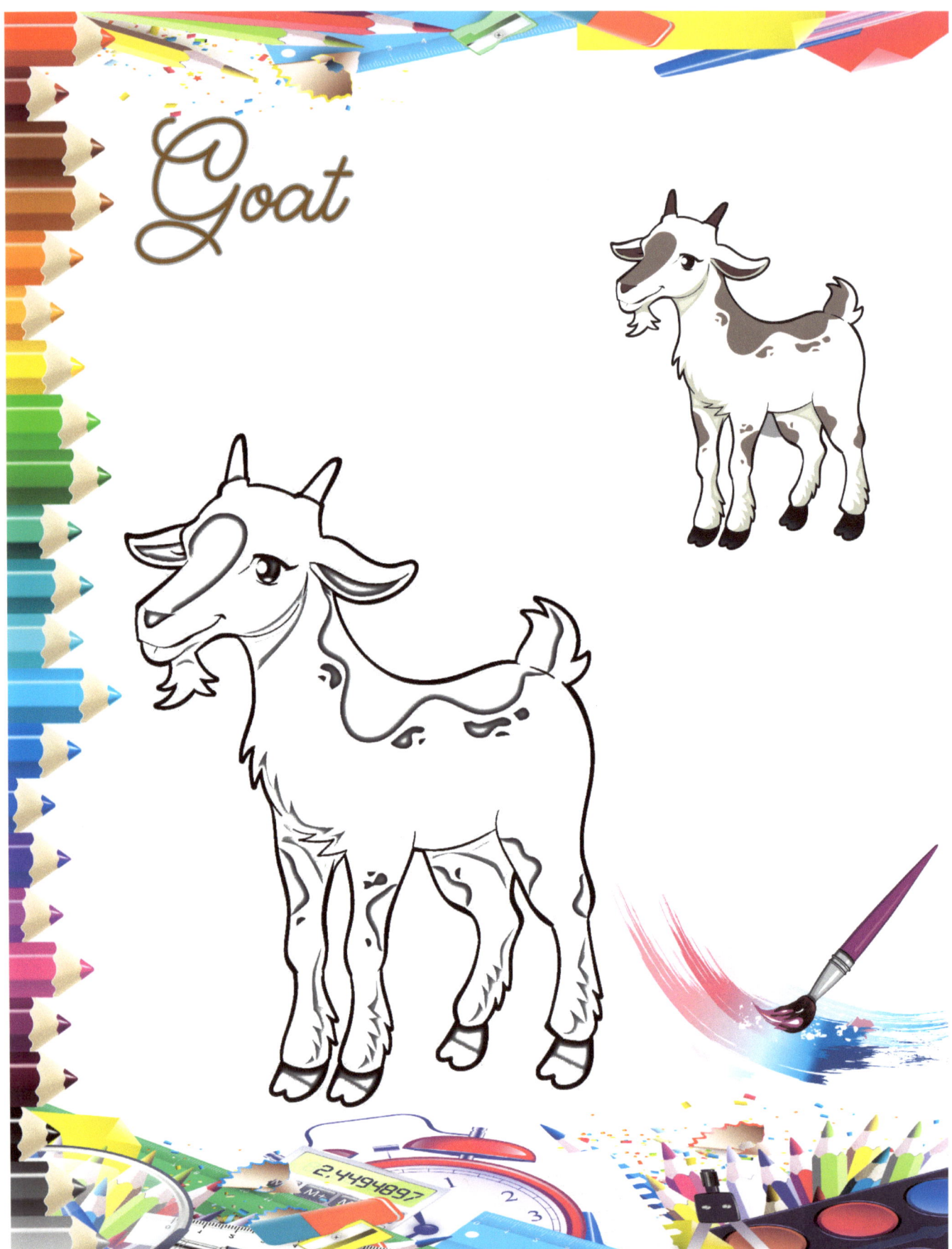

Duck

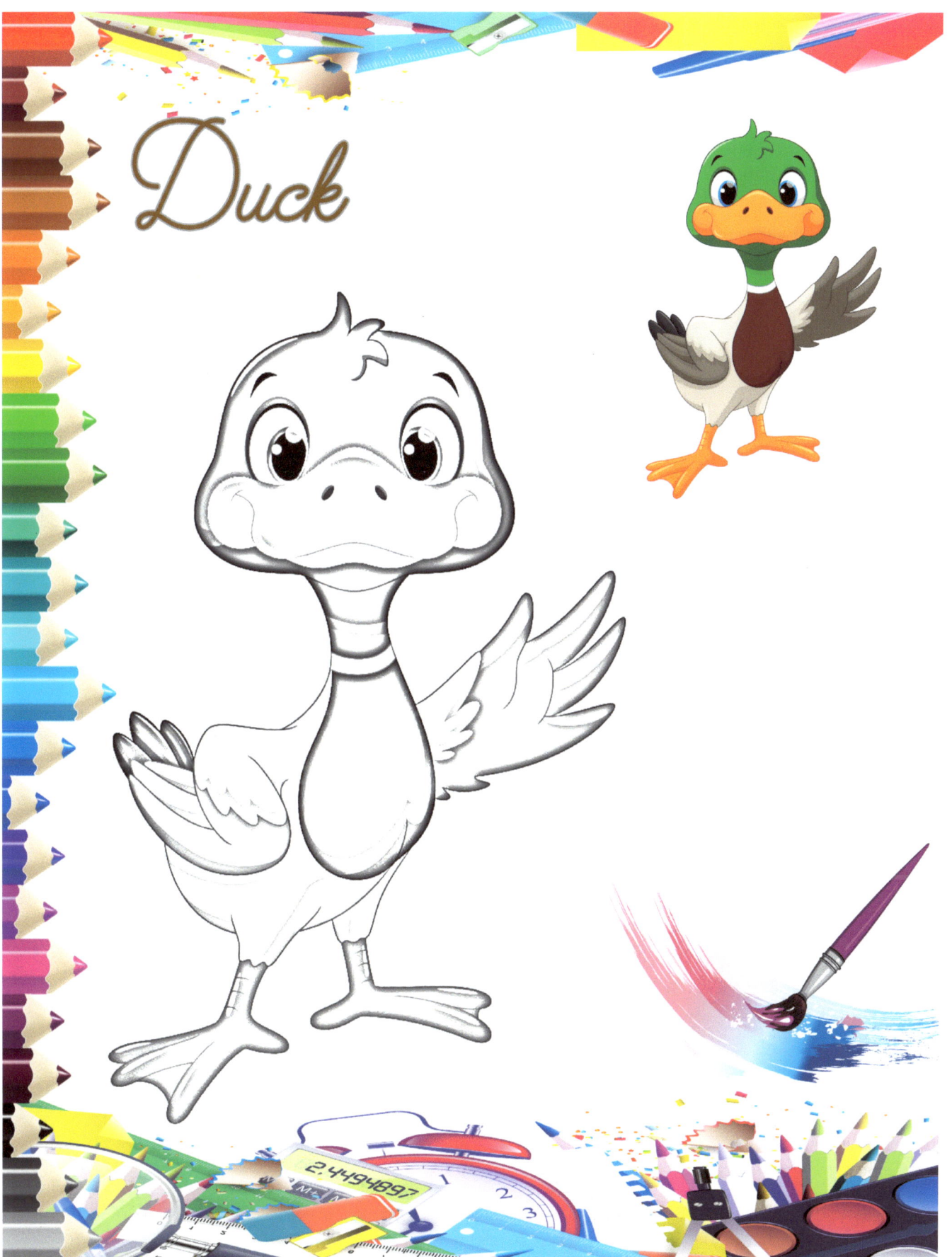

Fox

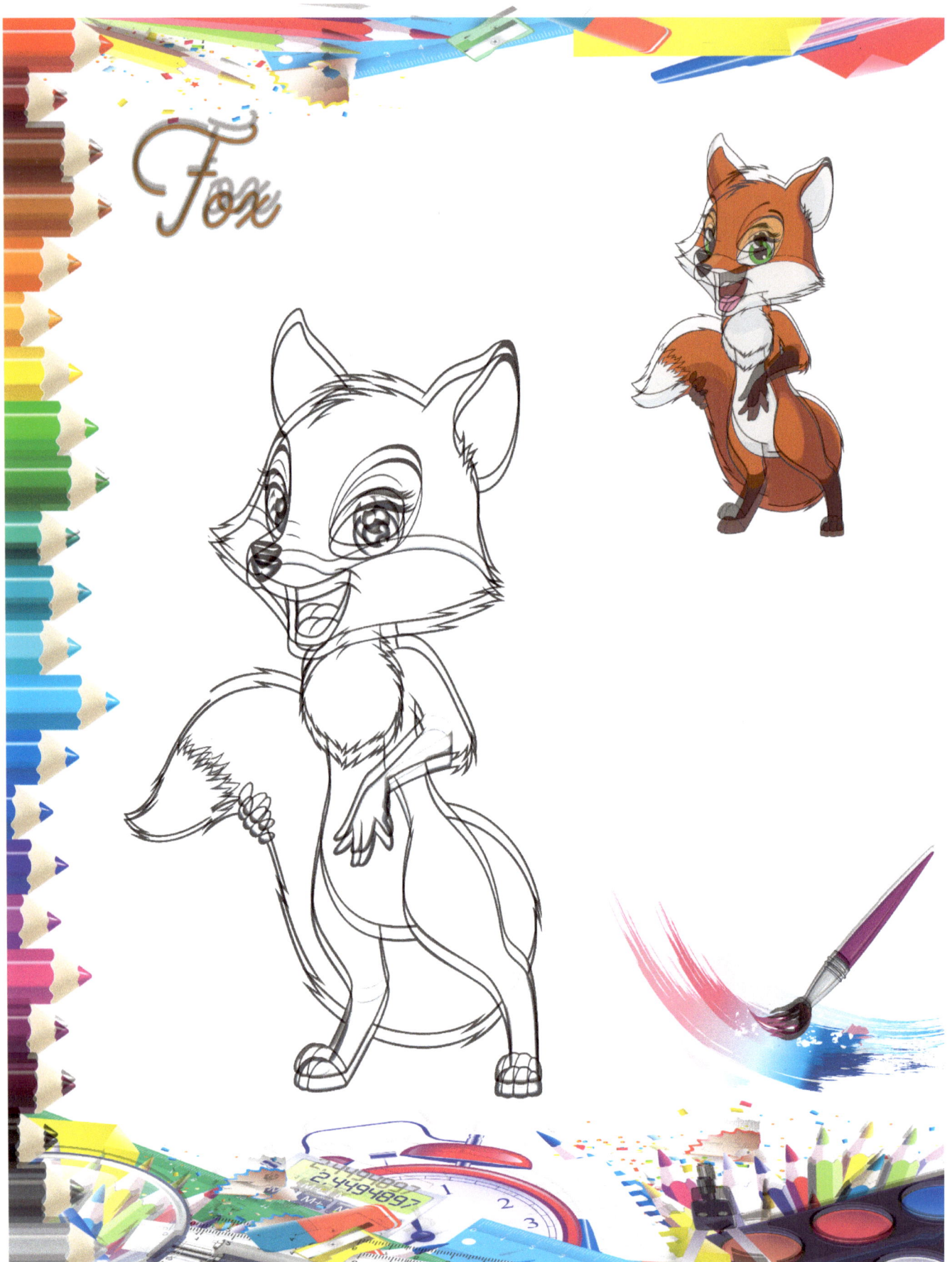

Bear

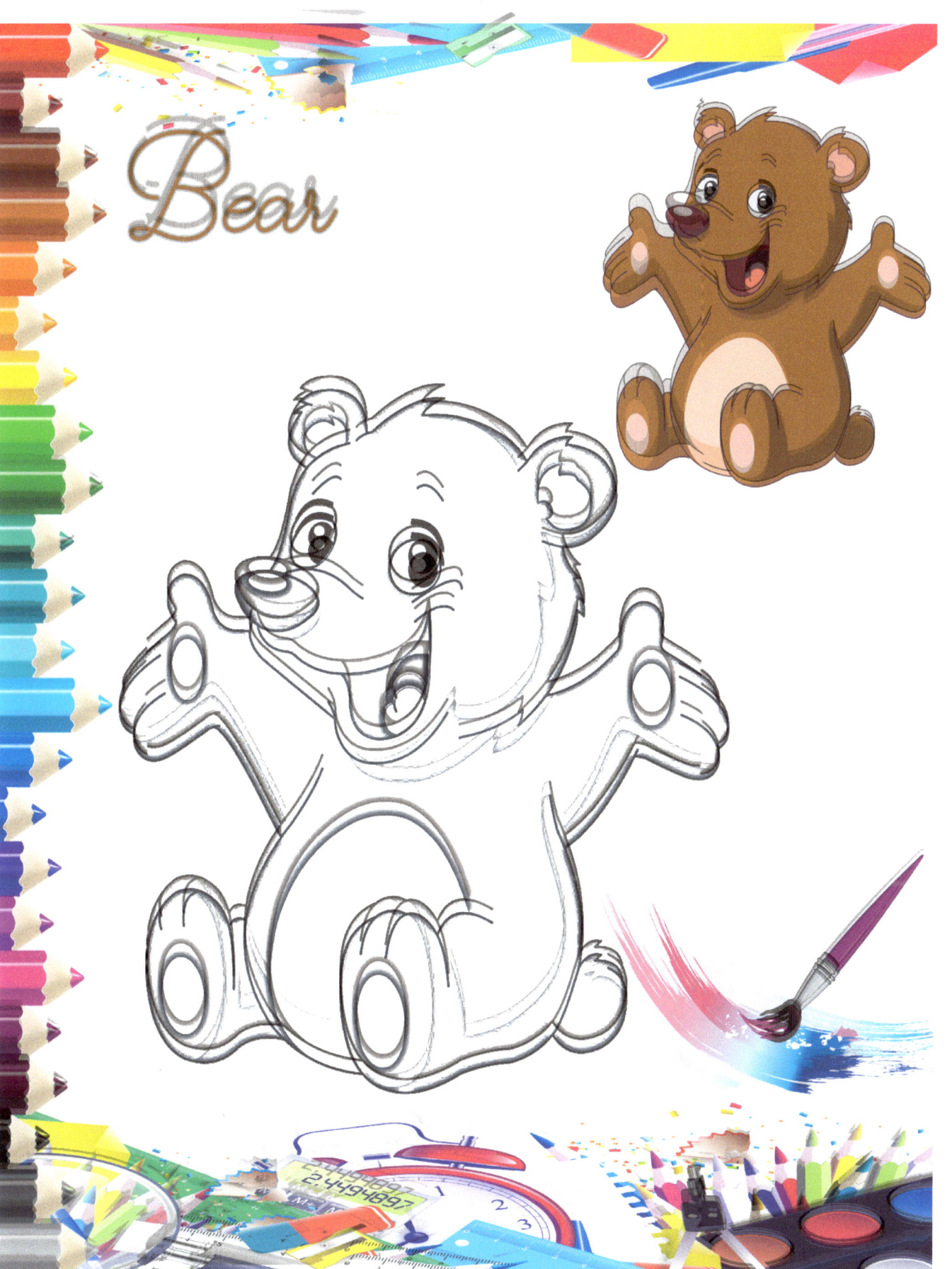

Crocodile

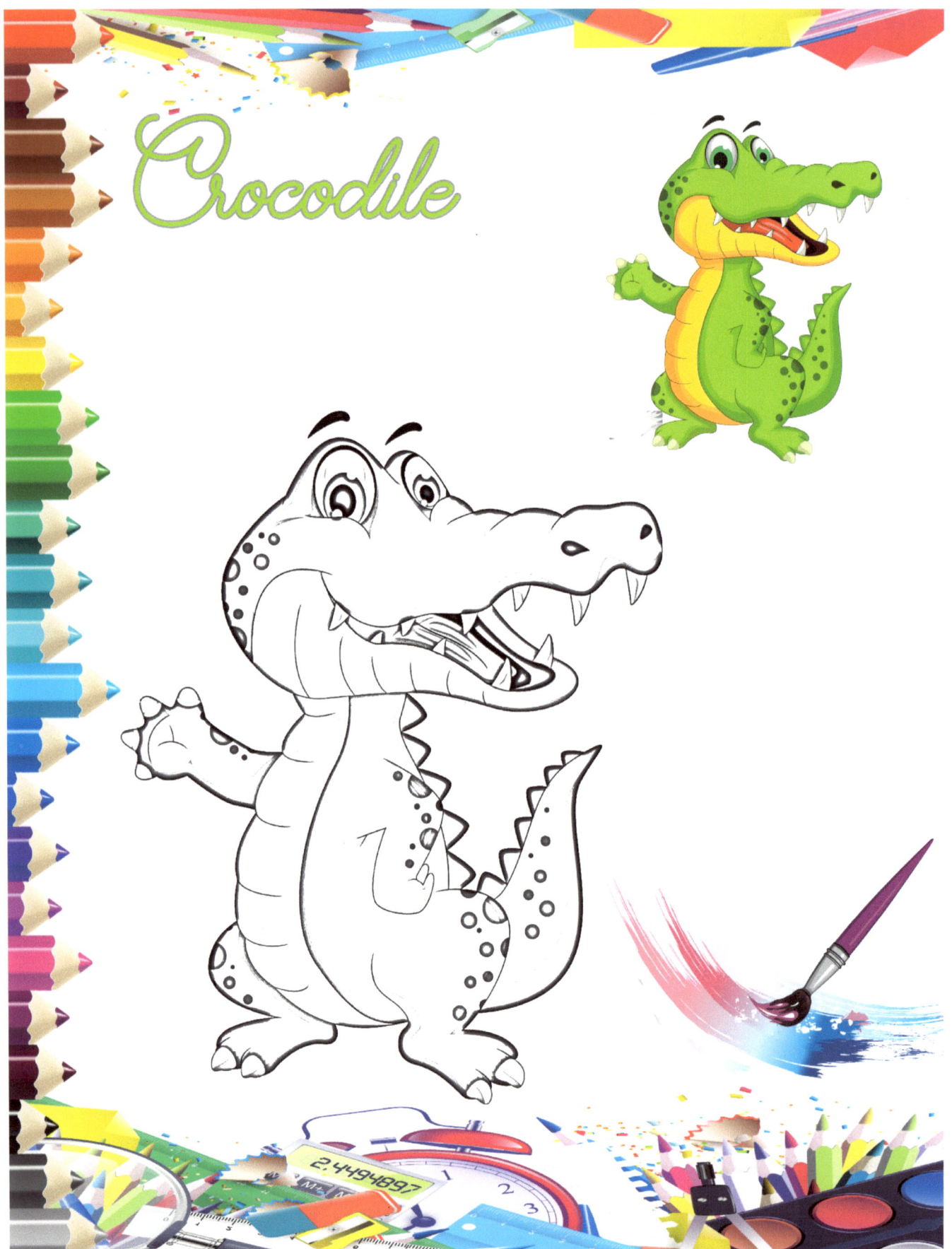

Tom & Jerry

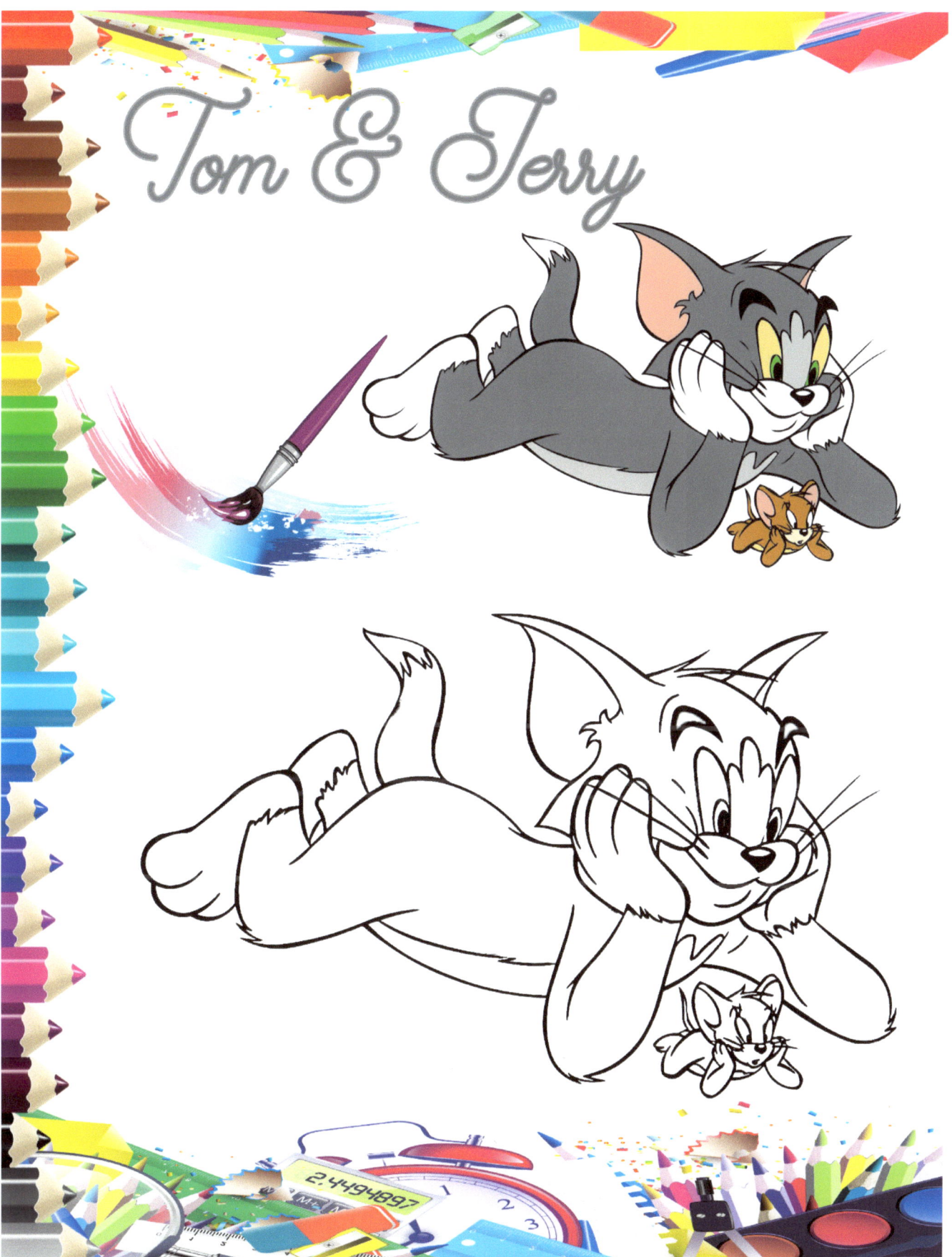

Dinosaur

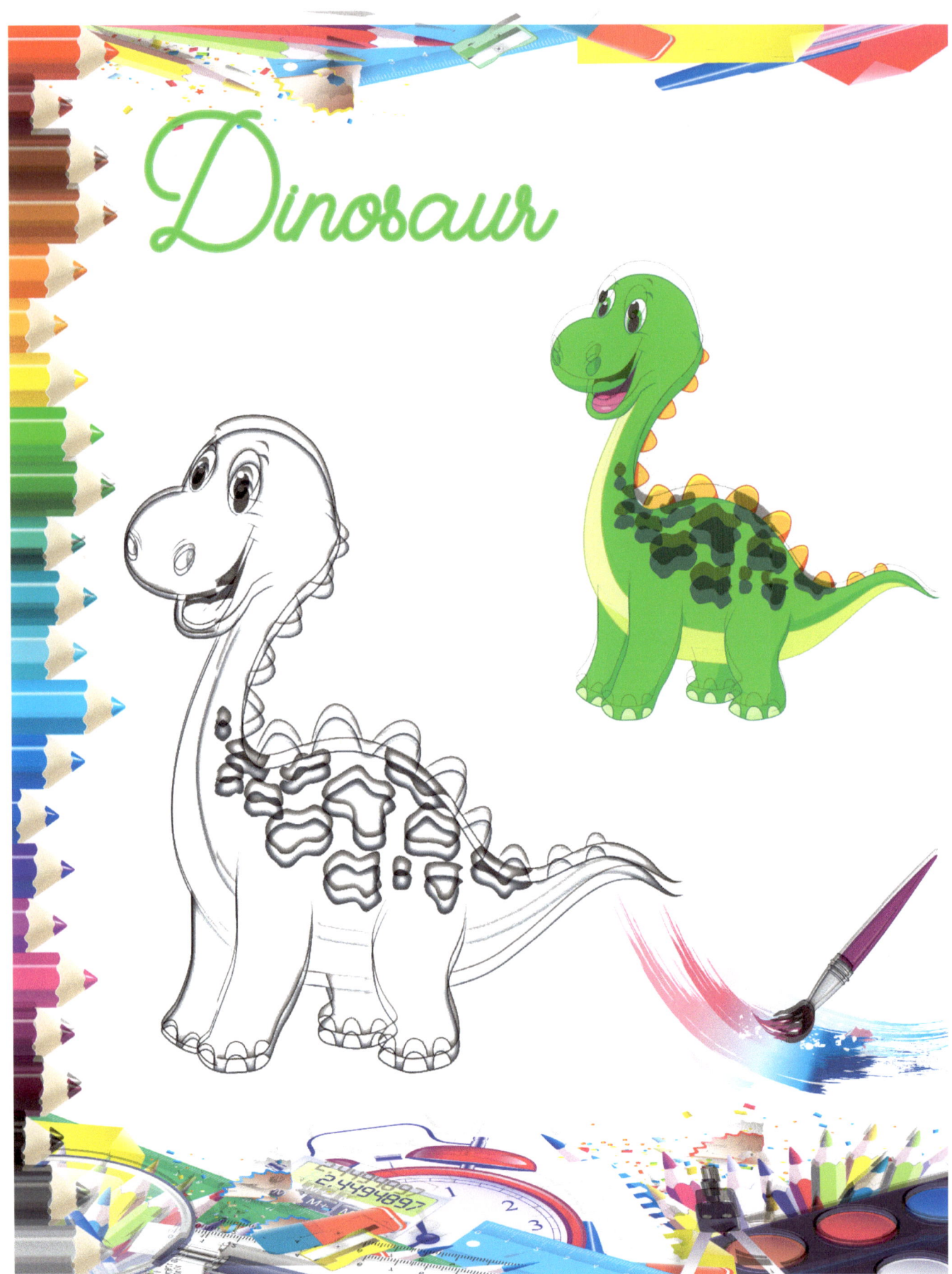

www.ingramcontent.com/pod-product-compliance
Lightning Source LLC
Chambersburg PA
CBHW051943210526

45473CB00006B/2360